ARENA
POCKET
GUIDE

ADVANCED

Western
Exercises

CHERRY HILL

D1405216

STOREY

Storey Books

The mission of Storey Communications is to serve our customers by publishing practical information that encourages personal independence in harmony with the environment.

Edited by Deborah Burns and Aimee Poirier
Cover design by Eugenie Delaney
Cover photographs by Richard Klimesh
Text design by Cindy McFarland
Production assistance by Susan Bernier
Line drawings designed by Cherry Hill and drawn
  by Peggy Judy

The information in this book is true and complete to the best of our knowledge. All recommendations are made without guarantee on the part of the author or Storey Communications, Inc. The author and publisher disclaim any liability in connection with the use of this information. For additional information please contact Storey Communications, Inc., Schoolhouse Road, Pownal, Vermont 05261.

Storey Books are available for special premium and promotional uses and for customized editions. For further information, please call the Custom Publishing Department at 800-793-9396.

Printed in Canada by Transcontinental Printing
10 9 8 7 6 5 4 3 2 1

Library of Congress Cataloging-in-Publication Data

Hill, Cherry, 1947–
  Advanced western exercises / by Cherry Hill.
    p.   cm. — (Arena pocket guide)
  ISBN 1-58017-047-1 (pbk. : alk. paper)
  1. Western horses — Training. 2. Western riding. I. Title.
  II. Series: Hill, Cherry, 1947– Arena pocket guide.
  SF309.34.H55 1998
  798.2'3—dc21   97-49048
                                                            CIP

Advanced Western Exercises

Arena exercises are a cross between gymnastics, meditation, and geometry. They are essential keys for discovering many important principles about training and riding.

Goals
- Fine-tune transitions and changes of direction
- Master lateral work
    Spiral
    Zigzag two-step
    Counter-flexed spiral in
    Rollback
    Sidepass
- Improve collection
    Small circle at the lope
    Lope and sidepass
    Lope to halt to 360 to lope
    Halt to lope
- Learn lead changes
    Counter-canter
    Flying change

Remember as you practice that it is the QUALITY of the work that is most important. It is a much greater accomplishment to do simple things well than it is to stumble through advanced maneuvers in poor form and with erratic rhythm. Keep your mind in the middle and a leg on each side.

How Can You Tell If the Work Is Correct?

1. Work regularly with a qualified instructor.

2. Ask a qualified person to stand on the ground, observe your exercises, and report to you what he or she sees.

3. Have someone record your exercises on videotape. Then watch the tape carefully using slow motion and freeze frame.

4. As you ride, watch yourself and your horse in large mirrors on the wall.

5. Without moving your head, glance down at your horse's shoulders, neck, poll, and eye during different maneuvers to determine if he is correct up front.

6. Ultimately, the key is to develop a *feel* for when things are going right and when they are going wrong by utilizing all of the above feedback techniques. Answer the following by feeling, not looking:

* Is there appropriate left to right balance on my seat bones? Can I feel them both?
* Can I feel even contact on both reins?
* Is the front to rear balance acceptable or is the horse heavy on the forehand, croup up, back hollow?
* Is the rhythm regular or does the horse speed up, slow down, or break gait?
* Is my horse relaxed or is his back tense?
* Is he on the bit or above or behind it?
* Is my horse loping on the correct lead?
* Can I tell when his inside hind leg is about to land?

What Do You Do When Things Go Wrong?

1. Review each component of an exercise.

2. You may need to return to some very basic exercises to establish forward movement, acceptance of contact, or response to sideways driving aids. Returning to simple circle work will often improve straightness and subsequently improve lateral work and collection.

3. Ride an exercise that the horse does very well, such as the walk-jog-walk transition. Work on purity and form.

4. Perform a simpler version of the exercise. If it is a lope exercise, try it at a walk or jog first.

5. Perform the exercise in the opposite direction. Sometimes, because of an inherent stiffness or crookedness in a horse, you will have difficulty with an exercise to the left but no problems to the right! Capitalize on this by refining your skills and the application of your aids in the "good" direction and then return to the "hard" direction with a renewed sense of what needs to be done. I often find that doing work to the right improves work to the left.

Large Circle — Small Circle

- Lope right lead.
- Lope the corner.
- Lope straight about 50 feet.
- Large circle to the right.
- As you return to the point where you left the rail, check your horse.
- Collect the lope.
- Lope a small circle.
- When you return to the rail, resume a normal lope and lope straight.

Try this at a walk or jog first.

Repeat the exercise several times in other parts of the arena and note the tremendous improvement by the third set of circles.

★ These circle exercises are a great means of developing speed control, collection, and balance.
★ Large circle — small circle is good preparation for Western reining maneuvers.

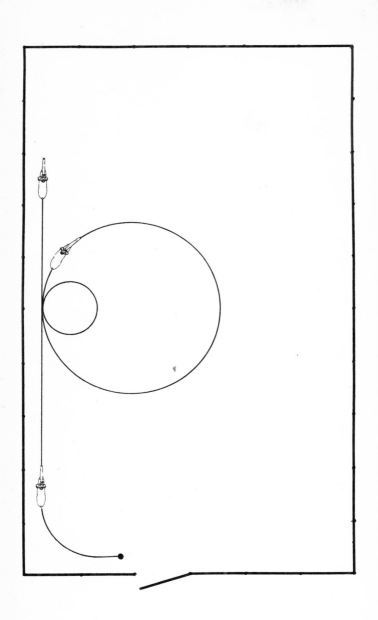

Spiral

- Jog a large circle to the right.
- Begin spiraling in.
- Maintain right bend using inside leg and rein if horse loses bend or slows down.
- Use outside leg to keep the hindquarters aligned.
- Inside shoulder back and outside shoulder forward.
- Weight inside seat bone.
- Use a slight opening rein on the inside and a neck rein on the outside (or just a neck rein if you are using a curb bit).
- Push with your outside leg at the cinch.
- Only go as far in as the horse is able to stay relaxed, in balance, and jogging in a proper rhythm.
- Then spiral out, maintaining the bend of the circle but applying the opposite aids.

- ★ First practice the spiral at a walk, but be careful to keep the horse's body aligned — no leg yield or turn on the hindquarters steps here.
- ★ At the lope, this exercise is very beneficial for conditioning the Western horse to lope small circles in balance.
- ★ Gets the horse listening to your aids on a circle.
- ★ Begins collection by working in smaller figures for a short time.
- ★ Can be used as part of a warm-up or a warm-down.
- ★ Don't lean your upper body into the spiral as if on a motorcycle because you will throw your horse off balance.
- ★ Don't let your horse slow down as you decrease the circle size.

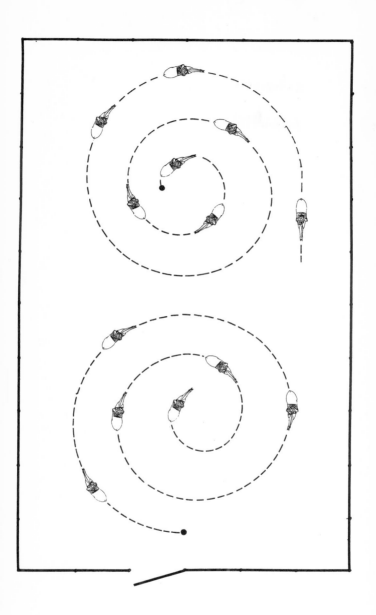

Counter-Canter across Diagonal

- Lope in a collected frame on the right lead down the long side and the short end to the second corner of the short end.
- Start a half circle to the right and then head across the short diagonal.
- Maintain right flexion (or even slight right position) even on the straight line.
- As you approach the opposite long side, check and prepare for a left turn in counter-canter (loping on the opposite lead to direction of travel).
  - Keep your shoulders parallel to the horse's shoulders.
  - Keep your pelvis parallel to the horse's hips.
  - Keep your weight deep in your left heel.
  - Bend the horse with your legs and keep your legs steady to help your horse keep his balance.
- Counter-canter a rounded square to the left.
- About two-thirds of the way up the long side, turn left and head across the short diagonal.
- Maintain right bend.
- When you reach the corner, ride the corner in a normal bend.
- After the corner, straighten.

In descriptions of counter-cantering, the terms *outside* and *inside* can be confusing. *Inside* refers to the shorter side of the horse, the one he is bent toward. In this exercise it is the right. *Outside* refers to the side that is longer — in this case, the left.

The rider's outside (left) leg must be very effective so the horse continues to lope forward with good impulsion.

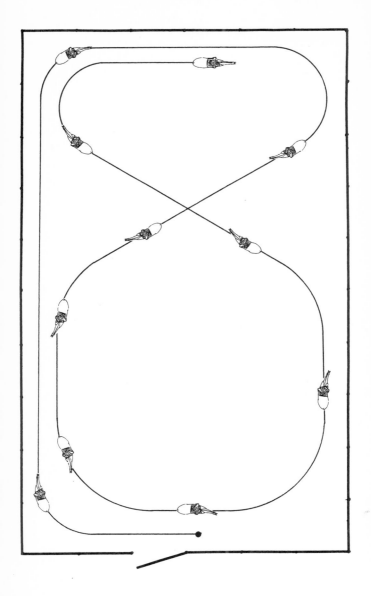

* A common error is the horse being too straight without any bending toward the lead.
* It is important that the rhythm be equal throughout. The speed on the straight lines should not be faster than that on the circular components.

Zigzag Two-Step

- Jog.
- Jog corner to the right.
- Jog straight 20 feet or so.
- Counter-bend left.
- Two-step to about 20 feet off the rail.
- Ride straight one stride.
- Counter-bend right.
- Two-step back to the rail.
- Ride straight, both corners of the far end.
- As soon as straight after second corner, flex left.
- Two-step to about 20 feet off the rail.
- Ride straight one stride.
- Flex right.
- Two-step back to the rail.
- Repeat sequence.
- Jog actively forward through the corner and across the gate end.

- ★ Practice this exercise at the walk first, asking for just a few steps at a time.
- ★ Try this exercise at both a walk and jog, riding the horse straight and with minimal flexion.

The two-step has a great deal more flexion and bend and more sideways movement than a leg yield. In either instance, the forehand should slightly lead the hindquarters.

Tests and improves the horse's response to forward/sideways driving aids. A good lead-in to sidepass.

Use a strong outside leg to keep the movement forward.

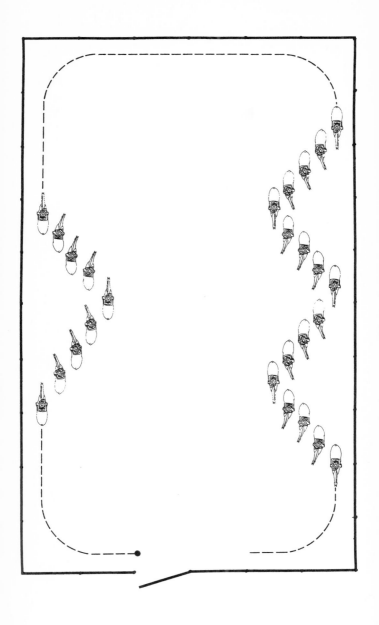

Counter-Flexed Spiral In

- Begin a large circle to the right at a walk with right bend.
- Follow a spiral pattern.
- At the halfway point of the first circle, change from right bend to straight.
- As you approach the starting point, change from straight to counter-flex with left flexion.
- Spiral in with the horse in the counter-flexed position.
- When you get to the center, you can ask for a few steps of counter-flexed turn on the hindquarters.
- Immediately straighten and ride forward out of the circle.

Since the hindquarters stay on the track, there is less crossover behind than in front.

Hold well with the right leg to prevent a sideways step of the right hind.

The counter-flexed spiral in is an easy way to teach a horse to move his front legs laterally and to cross over in preparation for pivots or turnarounds.

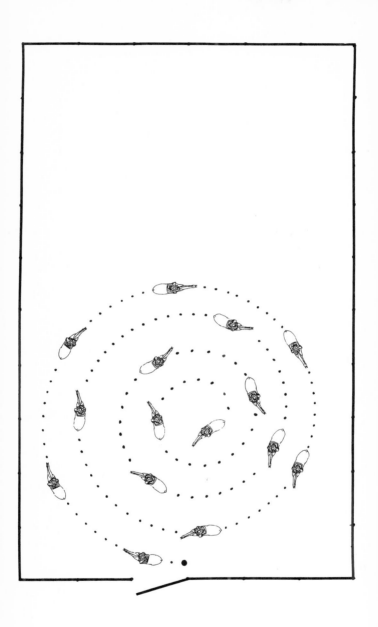

Rollback

- Lope right lead up the long side of the arena.
- Near the center of the long side, drift about 10 feet off the rail.
- Check several times to shift the horse's weight to his hindquarters.
- Without asking for a halt and with the forehand directly in front of the hindquarters, turn 180 degrees to the left.
  - Left rein to provide direction.
  - Right rein to guide the front end around.
  - Right leg to push the forehand sideways.
- After 90 degrees of the turn, release rein aids to prevent overturning.
- Lope left lead.

Variation: Practice at the walk and jog first to become familiar with the aids.

A rollback is described as a set and turn at a lope as opposed to a halt and turn or a sliding stop and turn.

Starting on the rail and then drifting off the rail is better than riding the whole exercise on a straight line that is off the rail. Drifting off the rail keeps the horse's body straight but aimed slightly to the right, which sets the horse up for a better rollback to the left.

Don't let the hindquarters swing to the right on the "set" or it will ruin your chances of planting the pivot foot (left hind).

Prevent overbend to the left by providing some positive resistance with the right rein, which keeps the horse straight and guides him through the turn.

During the turn, it is important that the inside pivot foot (left hind) bear the weight all through the turn, so that when the turn is finished, the right hind

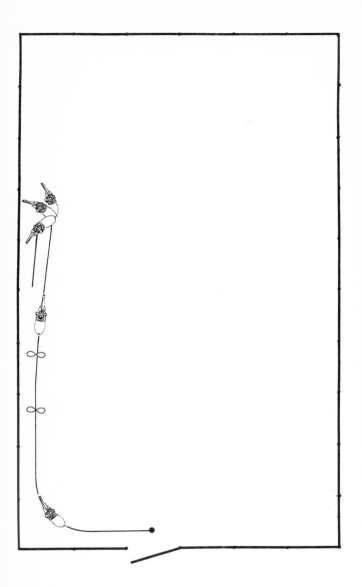

is free to initiate the left lead by driving off strongly as beat number one of the lope stride.

The rollback really shows a horse what balancing on his hindquarters feels like. When done properly, it can strengthen the loin and back, provided you don't strain the horse's hind legs.

Sidepass Variations

- Walk around the corner and up the long side of the arena.
- Once your horse is straight, turn on the forehand 90 degrees, with the horse flexed left and hindquarters moving to the right.
- When facing the arena rail
  - weight your left seat bone,
  - sidepass right 3–4 strides, modifying the aids for two-track to achieve a full sideways movement.
- With the horse still flexed left (counter-flexed), turn on the hindquarters to the right.
- Ride straight, then the corner.
- Ride one stride straight.
- Ride one stride flexed left.
- Turn on the forehand.
- When horse is facing the rail, straighten his body.
  - Sit evenly on both seat bones.
  - Sidepass to the right 3–4 steps, possibly using an occasional right opening rein.
- Flex slightly right and turn on the hindquarters.
- Ride straight, then corner, and straight.
- With right flexion, perform a turn on the forehand with hindquarters moving right.
- Retain right flexion and sidepass right 3–4 strides.
  - Weight right seat bone.
- Retain right flexion and turn on the hindquarters 90 degrees to the right.
- Straighten and walk forward.

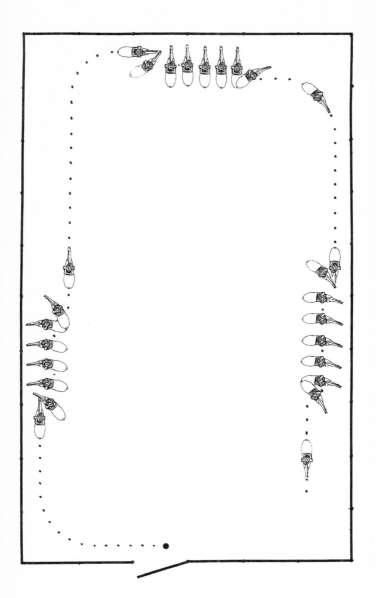

This group of exercises varies the flexion from left to straight to right in the turn on the forehand, turn on the hindquarters, and the sidepass.

Lope Large Circle with Sidepass

- Lope a large circle to the right on the right lead.
- At the arena center, halt.
- Sidepass to the right 2–3 strides.
- Lope left lead in a large circle to the left.
- At the arena center, halt.
- Sidepass to the left 2–3 strides.
- Lope right lead.

Keep the horse's body straight for the sidepass work, but flex him away from the direction of sideways movement.

This exercise sets the horse up for proper lope position from a standstill.

★ To prevent anticipation, vary the exercise by loping through the center of the figure 8 sometimes. Also, simple changes can be substituted for the sidepass.
★ Eventually, only sidepass one stride in the center.
★ Finally, substitute a flying change.

Note: Foot sequence in sidepass to the right is the same as the walk. Horse might start off taking a small step to the right with the right front.

1. Left hind crosses over in front of the right hind.
2. Left front crosses over in front of the right front.
3. Right hind uncrosses from behind the left hind and steps to the right.
4. Right front uncrosses from behind the left front and steps to the right.

Numbers 2 and 3 happen almost in unison, allowing the horse to retain his balance.

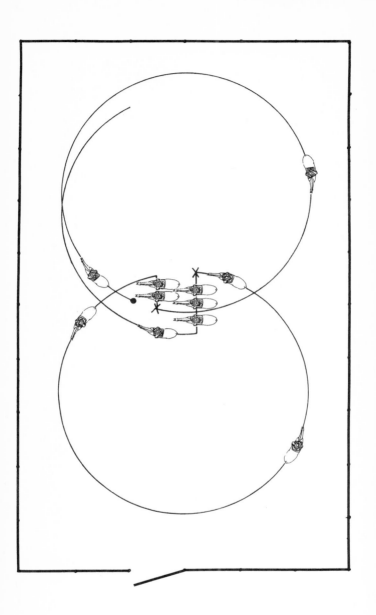

Lope — Halt — 360 — Lope

- Begin loping on the right lead.
- Lope straight about 20–30 feet.
- Check your horse and re-balance his weight to the rear.
- Make a moderately sharp turn to the right at least 20 feet off the long side.
- Lope straight ahead 60 feet or more, checking the horse with every stride.
- Double intensity check.
- Halt.
- Flex right.
- Perform a 360-degree pivot to the right at a walk with precision and slow-to-moderate speed.
- At about 340 degrees, lessen your left leg pressure and apply a right leg at the cinch to "catch" the turn to the right and to straighten the horse's body for the lope depart right lead.
- When facing the same way you began, lope right lead.

  Variations:
  - Lope out of the pivot on the left lead.
  - Perform the pivot to the left.

- ★ Remember, right flexion does not mean hind-quarters left!
- ★ This exercise allows you to teach and monitor straightness during corners and the pivot.
- ★ Practicing this exercise will show you if your horse stays balanced from left to right in a right turn.

If you let the horse overbend to the right or fall in on his right shoulder, it can cause his hindquarters to come "unstruck" and swing left.

Your horse must stay up on the left rein through-out the 360 even though he is bent slightly to the

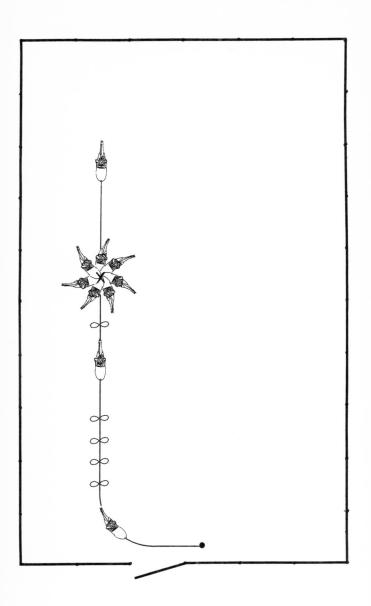

right, or he won't be in position to lope on the right lead after the turn. If you find he has lost his position, you may have to dramatically straighten him, pick him up, or even leg yield one step to the left to set him up before asking for the lope right lead.

Flying Change

- Lope 65-foot circle on right lead.
- Start across the diagonal with right bend.
- Straighten.
- Check (series).
- Before the flying change, prepare by:
  - performing a check;
  - changing very slight flexion to left;
  - moving your new outside leg (right) behind the cinch but letting it remain passive temporarily;
  - being sure your new outside rein (right) supports the left flexion;
  - hesitating new inside leg (left) in its old position, holding, to help keep the horse's body straight.
- Flying change at moment before suspension, as old leading foreleg (right) is swinging forward to land.
  - Use your new inside leg forward and active to engage new inside hind.
  - Ease new inside rein slightly to allow new leading foreleg to stride out.
  - Weight to inside seat bone without twisting.
  - Outside leg active behind the cinch to cause the new outside hind to jump well under and carry the horse's weight.
- ★ A flying change occurs during the moment of suspension between two lope strides. The former inside hind (right) becomes the new outside hind, the first to land and start the new lope, left lead.
- ★ Most horses change more easily from right lead to left lead. If right lead is more balanced than the left, ask for a left-to-right lead change first.
- ★ Flying changes are easier the more active and forward the lope.
- ★ Flying changes are easier and more correct the straighter the horse is before, during, and after the change.

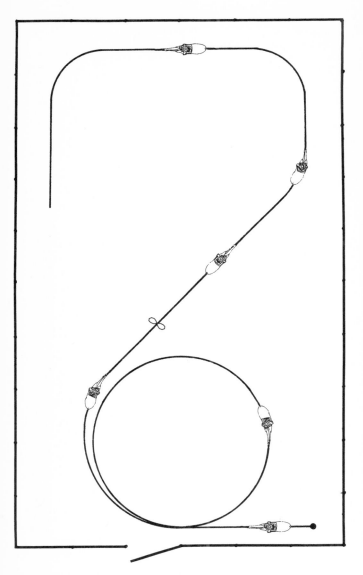

Only attempt a flying change after your horse is soft, supple, and solid and will perform balanced lope departs from a walk. He should also be able to counter-canter and perform precise simple changes with a certain number of walk steps.

Preparing for Your Test

Work regularly with a qualified instructor.

Practice all the exercises in this guide in both directions.

Visualize the test pattern, "ride" it in your mind. Draw the pattern on a piece of paper several times to be sure you know the order of maneuvers.

Practice individual portions of the test with your horse, but don't over-practice the actual pattern or your horse will anticipate. Anticipation leads to rushed work and errors.

Choose your examiner carefully. You may wish to use your regular instructor or another experienced rider, trainer, or instructor. If you ask someone inexperienced to evaluate you, you'll get unproductive results.

Make photocopies of the score sheet. Since you may want to ride the test several times, have extra copies of the score sheet available.

Arrange to have your test videotaped. Later you can compare the examiner's notes with your actual ride.

Rider warm-up. This is accomplished both in and out of the saddle.

Loosen up by giving your horse a vigorous grooming.

Test your suppleness as you squat down to put on your horse's boots or your spurs. If you are stiff, do some stretches before you mount up.

Once mounted, do a few upper body stretches, arm circles, leg swings, head rolls, ankle rotations, and leg and arm shakes.

Breathe. Throughout your warm-up and your test, be sure you are breathing regularly and properly.

Take air in through your nose, and send it down to fill your abdomen.

Exhale through your mouth to empty lungs and deflate the abdomen.

Especially when you are concentrating and focusing, be sure to breathe in a regular rhythm.

Horse warm-up. Just before the test, warm-up your horse.

Start out at a lazy walk on long reins so your horse can blow and stretch his back and neck and relax.

After a few minutes, sit deep, flex your abdominals, put your lower legs on your horse's sides, and gather up the reins.

For about ten minutes, walk or trot your horse along the arena rail, or make large figures such as 60-foot circles or large serpentines.

Let your horse have a little rest break on a long but not loose rein, as you walk for a minute or two.

Pick your horse back up and practice one or two of the transitions or a lateral or collection exercise from this guide.

Good luck! Ride the test well!

Circle, Simple Change, Flying Change

How to Ride the Test

- Lope a large circle to the right on the right lead.
- After you pass your starting point, walk for a stride.
- Lope left lead with left bend on the circle to the right (counter-canter).
- After you pass your starting point again, straighten and flying change to right lead.
- Change to right bend and lope a circle.

Test Ride Tips

★ In a flying change from left to right, the footfall pattern of the left lead is: the initiating hind (the right hind), then left hind with right front, finished by the leading foreleg (the left front).

★ During the flying change, when the old leading foreleg is on the ground, all other legs are in the air. The hinds are relatively even with each other in terms of height, flexion, and how far ahead they are.

★ Then the left hind, which was a member of the old diagonal pair, lands and becomes the new initiating hind. The right hind moves in front of the left hind as this occurs. The right front is already in front of the left front and is flexed.

★ The new diagonal pair (right hind and left front) is getting organized to land together but until they actually land, it appears that the hind will land before the front. When the diagonal pair actually hits the ground, though, the legs are in unison. However, the left front lands closer under the horse's body than it does in a usual lope stride, so the diagonal pair lands closer to each other during a lead change than they would normally.

★ The new leading foreleg, the right front, really

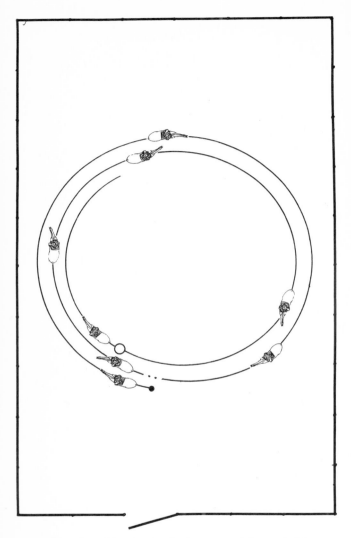

reaches ahead in the lead-change stride, and this is accentuated by the fact that the left front leg landed farther back than normal.

* In the lope stride following the lead change, the stride becomes normalized.
* Keep the circle very large at first. The smaller the circle, the more collected the lope must be.
* Maintain an even tempo. Don't slow during the counter-canter; don't rush after the flying change.

To the Examiner ...

You are performing an important role for the rider you are observing. Please study the test pattern carefully and know the exact instructions. Always strive to encourage, not discourage, a rider by your comments. Look for details that can help a rider improve. Try to determine whether it is the rider that needs help or if it is the horse that needs work.

The Numbers. *High scores:* There are so many things that can be improved in a horse or rider. If you give high scores right away, there is less room for improvement. *Low scores:* When you must give a very low score, offer at least one positive comment along with your suggestions for improvement.

Each maneuver is scored on a basis of 0–10

- 10 = excellent, perfect, took my breath away!
- 9 = everything was correct but lacked exquisite smoothness and brilliance
- 8 = good job, everything required was performed but overall it lacked finesse
- 7 = average job, performed correctly but lacked absolute smoothness, promptness, accuracy, evenness
- 6 = minor mistake such as horse bent incorrectly for a few strides or late transition
- 5 = one major mistake such as breaking gait for a few strides but then corrected, wrong lead for a few strides but then corrected
- 4 = two major mistakes made that were corrected
- 3 = three major mistakes made that were corrected
- 2 = one major mistake that wasn't corrected
- 1 = maneuver did not resemble test requirements
- 0 = didn't perform the maneuver

Comments. Be descriptive and creative with your comments — they will help the rider more than numbers because your words will stay in her mind. If you write "poor jog," it doesn't tell much, whereas "a stumble, quick rhythm at beginning of circle, hollow back and short stride" tells the rider much more.